LS | poems

LAUREN SUM is a musician, writer, creative and traveler of the world. She was born in Salt Lake City, Utah and graduated from the University of Utah with a Bachelor of Arts in Film and Media. Her work includes song and music video, *The Ghosts On the Lake* (2014) and now her self-titled collection of poems, *LS* (2016).

www.laurensum.com
Instagram/twitter: @lolovesmusic

ls poems

Copyright © 2016 by Lauren Sum

Cover Design and Photography by Lauren Sum

Hand lettering by E. Rhondeau Morgan

All rights reserved.

ISBN: 978-0692735435

www.laurensum.com

Printed in the United States of America

First printing, December 2016

"You must do the thing you think you cannot do."

(Eleanor Roosevelt)

CONTENTS

wood and wires   3
Steenbeck   4
Resistance   5
eight and a half   6
a thousand bangs and a heartbeat   7
madness   8
more than a bell   9
if only i could remember   10
red   11
nothing's ever going to break me   12
the wrath of god   13
the cost of happiness   14
this darkness   15
raw   16
immigrant   17
in the fob line   18
never understand   19
Tall Tales   20
the bricks of sugar   21
A divorce of sorts.   22
Medicine   23
Brutal   24
phantom limb   25
The Residents of the Glass House   26
the violet hour   27
blood orange moon   28
The ghosts were never there.   29
Under | GRADUATE | Post   30
the folly of men   31

There's only UP! 32
avant-garden 33
cult de sac 34
one hundred forty 35
kintsugi (no. 1) 36
kintsugi (no. 2) 37
Moondust 38
The ghost of Queenie Joan 39
Miss California 40
a hymn: the atom of all things 41
misheard (no. 1) 42
misheard (no. 2) 43
overboard 44
overheard 45
overlook 46
seeking his phantom 47
salt//saint//human 48
the fear of all that isn't there 49
circulatory/cursing 50
Cannibalized 51
Greed 52
para(phrased) 53
The Song of a Crooked Crow 54
What is music? 55
Guilin 56
We are Strangers in Paris 57
New York 58
MELBOURNE 59
20(16:9) 60
Keep Traveling 61

ls

poems

lauren sum

wood and wires

Wood and wires
Leaves and carpet
Organic and not so organic
Illuminated by a light bulb
A life arises
Entropy
Art.

Steenbeck

Steenbeck
Like Steinbeck
We become
Writers of our stories
Through a light and prism

Resistance

Resistance is a demon
Resistance is the reason
Another day goes by
With another blank canvas
Still white, not an inkling of colour

Resistance is family and a friend
Resistance is the voice
Telling me no,
Once again telling me lies,
Feeding me, "I can't" when I can

And I can.
And I really can!
And I really am
Made of art

So I sit
I go and DO
The WORK
I DREAM,
But mostly MAKE
And LIVE
Who I was made to be,
Who I was always meant to be

eight and a half

I'm 8½ feet under
I try to explain
But they steal my thunder

This ambition is sinking
When all I wanted to do
Was to be like Fellini

8½ and not under

a thousand bangs and a heartbeat

Click click click click
Tick tick tick tick
Tock tock tock tock
A thousand bangs
And a heartbeat
Of a machine
Rains and pours
In an infinite sound
Of entropic distress

madness

It's madness as I spin the thread
Mad like the Mad Hatter
I can't go to bed
'Til I find rhymes
So I can sleep again

The madness stings like a bee
This tiny creature landing on me
Multiplying its effect
And when I awake, I'll forget
The madness in me

more than a bell

The chiming of a bell
Overlooks and governs
The mundane necessity for order
In a universe of entropy

This noise of monotony
Seeks and destructs
The dreams of the land
To all creatures of the sun

More than a bell in an infinity
The bell is still and awake
In a dark matter of truth
What Pavlov knew

if only i could remember

If only I could remember
When I wrote the words,
"The parade is marching away
A final echo of the drums
All that was built
Falls down
Like Pompeii."

Sometimes broken poems march away.

red

flashing red lights
a runway
a siren
of terror and love
a district
a house
of mischief and crime
following me,
following me home

nothing's ever going to break me

Oh, that man's machine is a killer
Staring me down with her growling teeth
All shiny and new
But nothing's going to break me

My own brother laid down his whole life
For that killer of a machine
Made an oath signed in blood
I'm afraid he'll never come clean

They can pretend money
Will keep them sane
With a wretched white ghost on parade
That machine like a mistress of a maid

And I will deny my own blood
That man and his machine
Will never lay a hand on me
Because nothing's ever going to break me.

the wrath of god

Adam fell
That man might be
That man might know
Joy.*

That man, I couldn't conquer or become
Instead, a man of unforgivable error I became
Untruthful to myself, to a maker
With guilt burning heavy in the flames

And what I saw then
When the heavens rained down
Was not the devil, but a face
With a raise of a fist,
The wrath of God
Hence struck a chord through my teeth

---

* The first stanza refers to 2 Nephi 2:25 from The Book of Mormon.

the cost of happiness

There is a hardness,
A harsh cutting cold

Black in a reign
Of the unholiest wars

Broke and broken, she wears
The crookedest feet

How hushed and still,
And further she runs to her demise

Unfathomable,
A phantom on the land has she become
For such is the cost of happiness.

this darkness

this darkness
looked like the dress of a tower
a Wilhelm scream shouting shadows
creaking, creeping, sleepwalking
bellowing a blare, that television
beastly howling, beastly devouring
all the food
and i should have punched him
away...real soon

raw

You tear me to pieces
To find the human within
But I hide or at least try
To keep my burdens
In the darkness

I never tell
But sometimes the ice melts away
And my soul knows
A spirit is released
To another kindred soul
And reveals all that is raw and real

immigrant

I am an immigrant
In the land of the free, or so it seems
With well-worn brown leather shoes on my feet
Reminding me of Charlie Chaplin

A president smiles and winks
Shielded in glass, framed along a wall
Belongings on my back and suitcase in hand,
I know I am here

This is foreign, I hear yet do not understand
Visitor or resident in overwhelming numbers
I cannot comprehend, I did not imagine
Crossing an ocean into another

in the fob line

Is it a foreign objects battle
Or a fresh off the boat betrayal?
I can never escape and my blood begins to boil
When my feet touch the soil
In the land where I was born,
The land of the free
Except for those who look like me
In the fob line

One speaks in an Engrish accent
Another one talks slowly and repeats the obvious
    once again
The veins in me burst
All these synchronized, wild angry animals
The authorized and elected authority
In a one sided race against an Asian face
When the truth is, no man ever believed in "all men
    are created equal"
In the fob line

Look through an x-ray, then strip me of my
    belongings
Wear your gloves and search my bags with a look of
    disgust
While I remain quiet and all you see is disease
Written all over me, filled with vulnerability
As the enemy finds an excuse
To throw my beings in the dust
To write up a supererogatory fine
In the fob line

never understand

I suppose you'd never understand
If you've never seen the horizon
Across a nowhere desert sand

I suppose you'd never understand
If you've been turning up the noise
Thinking you were the better man

I suppose you'd never understand
If all you believe is what you've been told
So you never left your soil and land

Tall Tales

Tall tales, tall buildings
In the salt of the city
I told my brother,
"The lions live at the Lion House."

He looked round and around about
Then asked, "Where are the lions?"
To which I replied, "They're on vacation."

Tall tales, tall buildings
I was taller then
My brother is taller than me now
And now he tells
Tall tales

the bricks of sugar

the bricks of sugar
fill my eyes
of what was once
dirt and desolation
forgotten history
on the land

the bricks of sugar stand
in the sweetest tall glory
of all the sugar houses
and sugar fields
'til the birds stop singing back
'til the birds stop singing back

A divorce of sorts.

I DON'T WANT A YARD SIGN.
I want my freedom.
Freedom from this land.
A divorce of sorts.

I DON'T WANT TO WEAR YOUR NAME.
Or anyone's name in this town.
When it's all salt and fairweathered.
A discord well-worn and known at twenty-four.

Medicine

Poisoned.
By the lack of medicine.
They took it away, they took it away
And said, "You'll get addicted,
high and drinking in sin."
They left me in the dark
And nobody would listen.

My mouth wanted to shout
Obscenities.
But where was the doctor?
When my throat was heavy
And fell away to a throne
Getting owned
While they laughed

What can't be unseen
What can't be unfelt
All the medicine.
Now won't settle
All the wounds scarred.

Brutal

Brutal are the roots
From which we came

Brutal are the bruises
The ones we hide

Brutal is the brittle backbone
In the lost, not yet found

Brutal is maroon
In the heart of black

Brutal is the ghost
We've known and well worn

Brutal is the breath
Offbeat and in a struggle

Brutal nightmares
Brutal, brutally felt

phantom limb

How did it all begin with a telePHONE?
I inquired and you answered
Through the static and whispers
WHISPERS, WHISPERS, WHISPERS

I listened and heard
A herd of your honesty
And I was self-assured
I wouldn't need a warranty
But slowly, surely
I sent out a warrant
You weren't you or who
I thought you were
What we were
To be
Then I found out
How PHONY,
The infamy that you seek

Severed and scarred
All the wrongs settled into my bones
And now, I won't go on another whim
'Cause I don't feel
I don't feel anymore
Nothing
But my phantom limb.

The Residents of the Glass House

The residents of the glass house
Throw stones with their upper hand
Dictating with an elitist diction
So eloquent, so seemingly poised
Yet possessed
In a cult

the violet hour

in the violet hour,
violins croon with the crows
oh, there's sadness in the crimson
and the whitest whites i've ever known

a golden moon of a muse dances
in phosphor freckled flames
and light years ahead, she travels
across the ever caving echoes

blood orange moon

bewildered by the wild,
blood orange moon
clouded in hues, a ruse
a staircase

suddenly, the universe
whispered a tune
and waltzing were the stars
over the city lights,
all before dawn

The ghosts were never there.

I was once "Enthusiasm for Everything!"
Beckoning was an infinite sea
Which left me running to the shore
With such a surety
As if I had already known before

But when I reached the salt of a multitude,
There was nothing
Nothing, despite all those seeds
While traveling sleepless

Rushing were the waves
In reply of and crying,
"The ghosts were never there."

Under | GRADUATE | Post

I was an undergraduate
Who longed for the breaks,
Winter, spring and summer
Waiting to awake and say,
"LIVE LIFE NO. 21 Get Lost!"

Then four and a half years later,
I became a graduate
Ready to begin
Ready to live life again

And then I became a postgraduate
No longer dependent on the seasons
But still longing for that break

the folly of men

Scrutinise the mother
Scrutinise the teacher
Scrutinise the musician
Scrutinise the filmmaker
Scrutinise the writer
Scrutinise the missionary,
The bishop and holy order
The nighttime bartender,
The waiter and waitress,
The janitor
Those dreamers, those seekers
Those doers

Relentlessly and critically
Declared by others:
Unemployed

"You are not real unless you are
A Paid Working Mother
An Ivy League Professor
Beyoncé. Taylor Swift.
Steven Spielberg.
Stephen King. J.K. Rowling.
Not religious
Not a bartender
Not a waiter or waitress;
Certainly not a janitor."

Such foolish words
And such is the folly of men

There's only UP!

when you live
in the air

your head
stays UP there, too

bruised and lost
holes and knots

i howled, "darling, come back
down."
but there's no sound in space

avant-garden

can you hear the gods?
those heavenly creatures
of the earth
orchestrating an overture

saint-like tulips,
avant-garden

a landscape awakens
from a tired winter's sleep

cult de sac

So obscene
It's all I've seen
The bourgeois bagel
Cult de sac

one hundred forty

We're all April Fools!
Everything is a MacGuffin
Then I fixed it in post
"Mamma Bess, Mamma Bess"
Sometimes all you need is mindless pop;
A Wilhelm scream, all comical
"I'm starting to have Konichiwa Fever"
How I miss foley and the Frankenstein room
Songs about California never get old
It's love letters and it's madness, unrequited love
"I'm more of a whisper."
I've never felt more like a missionary in monsoon
    rains
Wearing the FUTURE and The Weatherman!
Music reminds me: calloused fingers, not a
    calloused heart
So long to German facebook
I have an Australia separation anxiety
"I'm capable of saying it sober."
C'est difficile, le musique
Reminiscing on choir days, especially when people
    fainted
Rendering. It goes on and on...
My life depends on caffeine
I spent my night with Steenbeck
All for the love of film

kintsugi (no. 1)

the world,
the Internet

a visit to a
residence

kintsugi (no. 2)

It's all been done before
I'm reminded of this
On an unknown
Unpaved coastal road
Cold and frantic
Across the world

But soon
We were more humble
Grown up from years before
Eager to unearth

Moondust

I fear, my Lord
This isn't Eden
Look across the landscape
The houses don't speak
And the strangers are the strangest
On Valentine's Day;
The dead air kisses and caves,
Towers pop! And delay...
There's a quiet broken man,
A broken cassette, a sleepy silhouette
Whose tracks travel the tunnels
With laughing, living
Moondust

The ghost of Queenie Joan

The ghost of Queenie Joan
Whistled to me, in the west, unexpectedly
In a second hand storeroom as the second hand
    turned south
I took a hint at the signs, listening
Listening to the engines, for a second chance
To rise from the vintage dust
1961

Queenie Joan closed her eyes, whiskey and cigarette
    in hand
How the smoke seemed to hold her glory days
She turned to me with the faint of a smile
And said, "Never leave, never leave.
For this dark red is a true saint."

Distilled in me, her stories worn weathered and well
Left me strumming, strumming to a song
Inherited and borrowed from
The ghost of Queenie Joan

Miss California

standing there, blazin' in shades
a subtle orange from submersing
in all kinds of plastic baked LA
salmon scrubs and grey sterile gloves
smoking on a cigarette
Miss California is out for the day
she isn't really there
but fading
to up and away...

a hymn: the atom of all things

reverent lines and winter light
holy hallelujahs
those wordsmiths write
found framework
and unearthed museums
here, the tidal waves of laughter
and humble heroes sing
a hymn: the atom of all things

misheard (no. 1)

Living here
With the rent so high
Now, we just buy herbs

misheard (no. 2)

down in the hollow
the universe rained again
fistfuls in the sea

overboard

I exclaim, "I am
an artist in the closet.
Close to being gay."

overheard

He says, "It's ok.
I'm the gay one in the family."
And together we laugh

overlook

From the overlook
We are magical thinking
It's almost LA

seeking his phantom

with all these years reeling
it's death 'til us part
the death of me
a magnitude

salt//saint//human

from the lookout,
we populate the stage
with synthetic sorrow
a self-delusional madness
of unconquerable conquerors

lacquered lachrymose
and a laughing laugh
oh, what we lack the most

yet like a hull housed rib cage
against the ribbon wind
we somehow become
a kind of saint – mortal immortalities

the fear of all that isn't there

regret is mourning
feeling the forgotten
country

destruction, progress
failure, fear
of all that isn't there

circulatory/cursing

The words came out of me:
Circulatory system
I was outnumbered.

And there I was
immersed
in the discourse of
a French pool,
Cursing the tower of Babel

Cannibalized

That was surely barbaric
A fight or flight kind of panic
What we witnessed in the dark
At the Barbican

But now I've been cannibalized
By that desperate manic
That dreadful miser
Unforgiving and a liar

Oh, I've been cannibalized
And now I realize
Flesh and bone
Blood and skin
How all the terror is real
But not the exhibition

Greed

It's the Season of Tweed
See the blazers blazing across the page
In the magazines
But it's Fashion Week in New York City
And everyone's wearing jeans

I went out searching for this tweed
And it looked like everyone was smoking weed
How could no one see?
The greed in tweed
And all these designer things

Sewn stitches all pretty
Made by people behind machines
The sign said "Handmade"
But all I could see was a manmade
Feed of exploitability

A lump sum of thousands to be paid
But none for the thousands to be freed
From the chain of chains
Rage! Rage! I want RAGE! Outraged and
    heartbroken
For not even minimum wage and the wagers of men

para(phrased)

                paralyzed
    and   paranoid
  by the   paranormal

i'm reminded
this isn't a   Paramount
Pictures
horror film

but a seeming   paradoxical
                      paradise

for phantoms

The Song of a Crooked Crow

I can hear the desert again
Burgundy, black, arroyo
The song of a crooked crow
And the creaking veins of a mill
Somewhere in Valentine
Their vacant fields whistle
While a traveler on the tracks
Steal a punch in the air
And those jagged teeth, how they laugh
With all those skeletons I drive past;
Such is a sacred stillness,
Such is a sort of sadness
As I leave the desert behind

What is music?

I want to know
music.

I want to know
"What is music?"

If music is...

The resonating strum
Through the drum
Of an old gasoline tin can

Getting unnaturally high
My mother and friend
Singing Chinese opera
From a soundproof basement

A cult of a chorus
Dancing to a deafening
Thunderclap of distortion

Some muse of a mountain
Some saint of a captain
Waving hands in the dust
For sparks. *Sparks!*

What is music?
What is music!
What is
music?

Guilin

spontaneous
rusted buildings
concrete sky
children running
the city on motorbikes
5 pm and school's out
yellow hats
rubble
the bus rumbles
red lanterns in the trees
firecrackers in the air;
the ringtone of an American Idol

We are Strangers in Paris

We are strangers in Paris

Lost in the night
You asked for directions
And I could only reply, "Je ne sais pas."

Enchanted and in love
With the city lights
Merci beaucoup, French gentleman!
For being my tour guide
Je suis désolé for running off in a fright.

Looking for romance
At the wrong arc de triomphe
On Champs-Élysées
Un homme high and drunk
Flirts with me, in front of my mum

Waking and walking dans la rue
Je ne parle pas français
Et vous ne parlez pas anglais
Yet, we walk together
As you kindly lead the way to Shakespeare

We are strangers in Paris
Et je t'aime

New York

Concrete faces, concrete souls
Reckless, heartless
New York

Oh, how I dreamed of the city
Yet wandered lonely
Riding the subway,
Hearing "Marching Bands of Manhattan"
And "Welcome to New York"

But what I didn't hear then
Haunts me now

How New York will always be there
But not the ones you love.

MELBOURNE

Meet me at Flinders Station, Federation Square or
    The Forum
Everywhere or anywhere in this southern
    hemisphere
Let's have lamingtons for breakfast and listen to
Buskers on the street, that busker playing Bon Iver
Oh, how my heart sings! Queen Victoria and Rose
    Street
Urban art down Degraves and Hosier
Ripper iced chocolate and parmas at the pub
NGV and the Costco Docklands, all the while
Exclaiming, "I wish I were an Antipodean."

20(16:9)

a thesis, a series
of focus pulling
the new year
4K resolutions
rendering, reeling
in flicker and frames;
(cinema)cartographers coding
20(16:9)

Keep Traveling

Sometimes,
I think I'm more lost
In my own city
Than abroad

Maybe home is calling
From all ends of the earth

And maybe I'll run away
Like the lines on a map
Running wild, running free

To keep traveling,
Keep traveling

ACKNOWLEDGMENTS

I would like to thank my mum/dear best friend/Mama Bess, Mingmee Sum. Thank you for carrying me with you on trips around this universe, teaching me how to be human and for all your infinite love and support. I am grateful for inheriting your sense and spirit of writing through the Mui ancestors.

Thank you to Morgan Jones for your kindness and for being my first reader.

Thank you to Dustin Schwindt and to all my Crooked Crow friends, especially Johann Wagner, Todd Russell Hall and Jordi Baizan. Thank you for helping me to write and believe in myself again.

To all my family, friends, heroes and everyone reading this, I HEART YOU.

www.ingramcontent.com/pod-product-compliance
Lightning Source LLC
Chambersburg PA
CBHW020959090426
42736CB00010B/1380